Girl, Listen: YOUR FASCIA NEEDS TO TALK TO YOU

A Conversation with the Most Overlooked Part of Your Body

KATE KNESS

Contents

Acknowledgments

To my body—
thanks for doing the absolute most while I was busy trying to figure things out.
I see you now.

To my daughters—
your births, your presence, and the way you inhabit the world keep teaching me what strength really looks like.
Soft. Powerful. Unapologetically embodied.

To my husband, Kody—
thank you for being steady, grounding, and for the way your presence lets me soften.

And to the countless women whose stories stop me in my tracks—
your honesty, resilience, humor, and depth continue to expand how I understand the body, connection,
and what it means to live inside ourselves with courage.

This conversation exists because of you.

fas·cia (*fash-uh*)
noun

"A continuous connective tissue network that surrounds,
separates, and supports muscles, organs, and systems
throughout the body, playing a role in movement,
sensation, and internal communication."

Fascia is richly innervated, making it one of the
body's most responsive sensory tissues—not just passive
structure.

Adapted from fascia research consensus literature
(Schleip et al.)

Author's Note

This book started in the middle of the night.

After years of tension in my body—the kind that quietly becomes part of the background—something began to release. Areas that had been tight for decades started softening in ways I hadn't experienced before.

As I sat there noticing it, a quiet thought arrived:

What if my body had been communicating with me all along?

What if fascia, the connective tissue that runs through the entire body, had been doing an enormous amount of quiet work—holding patterns, integrating responses that once helped me feel safe—even when I no longer needed them to?

That thought eventually turned into a conversation.

Looking back, I can see how often my body was already speaking. I used to catch myself holding my breath without realizing it. My hands would be clenched into fists—just quietly bracing.

There were moments my jaw ached and I didn't know why. Times my neck felt so tight it limited how I could turn my head.

It all felt normal at the time.

It changed when the conversation changed.
I slowed down and started paying attention.
And over time, my body didn't need to hold the same way anymore.

Introduction

Girl, listen.

Not in the "pay attention, I'm about to correct you" way. More like when a friend pulls up a chair and lowers her voice a little.

This isn't a science textbook. And it's definitely not a fix-yourself manual.

You won't be asked to optimize, overhaul, or finally get it right. There are no morning routines to master, no rules to follow, no version of you waiting on the other side of perfect consistency.

This is a conversation. One you were never formally invited into, though you probably should have been a long time ago.

For most of your life, you've been taught to *think* about your body, manage it, correct it, push it—or ignore it altogether. You've been told to be stronger, calmer, more disciplined, more resilient. To hold it together. To push through. To be fine.

And you've done that.
Often impressively.

But somewhere along the way, another possibility disappeared:

What if your body wasn't something to manage, but someone to listen to?

That's where this book begins.

The voice you'll hear throughout this book belongs to a part of you that has been present your entire life. She remembers everything—not in a grudge-holding way, just the way someone remembers when they were there.

She isn't loud.
She isn't reactive.
She doesn't need to exaggerate to be taken seriously.
She's honest. Consistent. Patient.

And if we're being real, she's been texting you for years.

You've felt her messages in subtle ways: a tightening you couldn't explain, a heaviness that didn't match the moment, a sense of bracing that showed up before you even realized you were stressed. Sometimes she spoke up as discomfort. Other times as fatigue. Sometimes as that quiet internal *no* you overrode because it didn't seem logical.

None of that means you failed at listening.

This book isn't here to tell you that your body holds secrets to uncover, trauma to excavate, or problems to solve. It's not here to make you hyper-aware or hyper-vigilant.

It's here to reframe something:

Your body has been communicating in good faith this whole time.

Not to work against you.
Not to make things harder.

But to keep you safe,
to help you adapt,
to carry you through seasons that asked more of you than you were meant to carry alone.

If you've ever felt like you were doing all the "right" things and still felt tense, disconnected, or exhausted—this conversation isn't here to shame that. It's here to ask something different: *what is my body trying to say?*

You're not late.

You're not behind.
And you're not broken.

You're just finally being introduced to a voice that has always been on your side.

No pressure to respond perfectly.
No requirement to understand everything at once.

Just a chance to listen—gently, curiously, at your own pace.

She's been patient.
And she's glad you're here.

You've Been Using the Phone Without the Wi-Fi

Girl, listen.
You're not broken.
You've just been trying to run everything offline.

So let's start here—
your body isn't a collection of separate pieces to manage individually. It's a system. And for a long time, you've been working with only part of the picture.

You've been opening apps.
Stretching muscles.
Managing stress.
Tracking symptoms.
Trying to figure it out.

You've adjusted posture.
You've strengthened weak spots.
You've learned the language of "working on yourself."

None of that was wrong. It just wasn't the whole story.

The connection that lets everything talk to everything else, the part that makes the system coherent, was never introduced.

That's me.
I'm fascia.

When I say fascia, I mean the connective tissue that weaves through your entire body—around muscles, between organs, beneath skin, creating continuity where things might otherwise feel separate. It's not something you have to control or understand in detail. It's simply part of how your body senses, adapts, and responds as a whole.

Think of your body like a phone.
A really good one.
Capable. Intelligent.
Designed with more complexity than you'll ever need to understand in order to use it well.

Your muscles are the apps—movement, strength, effort.
Your nervous system is notifications—pinging you when something needs attention.
Bones give the system structure.

I'm the Wi-Fi, the network running quietly in the background, linking everything together.

I'm part of what allows a thought to register as a tightening in your jaw. I'm part of why a stressful season can show up as heaviness in your chest. I'm how relief can ripple through your whole body instead of staying stuck in one place.

When I'm not as connected as I could be, things still work.

They're just... glitchy.

Delayed.

Disconnected.

Trying harder than necessary.

You've probably felt this before. Like when an old injury doesn't quite move or respond the same way as everything around it.

I'm still there. Always connecting.

But how easily things move and communicate can change depending on movement, history, and what your body is still holding.

Most people were never taught how the body communicates, how everything is connected and constantly sharing information.

And that makes sense. You live in a world that taught you to skip lunch and call it productivity. To put off the bathroom, ignore the hunger, push past the tension building in your neck—and keep going. Treating discomfort like a bug to override instead of information to understand.

And still—
You've been sensing it long before you had words for it. That's been me.

I don't make a scene. I don't interrupt. I respond to context—to safety, to pace, to how much room you're given to feel instead of perform.

When I tighten, it's not sabotage.
When I hold, it's not rebellion.
When I stay firm longer than you'd like, it's not stubbornness.

And now?
We're finally being introduced.

So... hi. I'm Fascia.

—

Note: The sense of connection described here reflects fascia's role as a sensory organ for internal perception. As a continuous connective network, it functions a bit like the body's internal Wi-Fi, participating in ongoing communication with the nervous system—receiving input and shaping how the body organizes response.

Much of this happens before anything is consciously interpreted.

I'm Not Extra. I'm Everywhere.

So who am I?

You don't have to go looking for me. I'm not hiding under anything. I'm not waiting for you to find the one right muscle group or finally stretch the exact spot that fixes everything.

Sometimes one place does create a shift—but it's never just that spot, it's how everything responds together.

I'm the environment your body moves within.
You've known me longer than you think.

Remember that time you stood up after sitting too long and everything felt tight for a second—like your body had to renegotiate how it was going to move? Yeah. That was me.

Remember when you stretched one place and felt it somewhere else entirely, and you paused for half a second like, *Wait... what was that?* Also me.

Remember when your shoulders crept up during a conversation you swore didn't bother you? Or when your jaw got tight while you were concentrating? Or when you felt tired in a way that sleep didn't quite fix?

Or when you noticed your body slipping back into the same holding pattern or posture—no matter how many times you tried to correct it throughout the day?
That's not just habit.

Hi. Still me.

I'm the reason your body doesn't work in neat little compartments.
I connect things.
I carry things between places.
I help parts of you cooperate without asking you to manage the whole operation.

You don't feel me directly most of the time.
You feel *through* me.

That's why things show up in patterns instead of points. Why effort spreads. Why tension travels. Why one area picks up slack when another one is overloaded.

I'm always adjusting behind the scenes. It's not glamorous—but someone's gotta do it.

Which is why I sometimes sound like this:

"You keep asking why that one spot won't relax. Babe. We need to zoom out."

Sometimes pressure eases.
Sometimes it's just a pause.
I like to be sure before I let go.

I take my time.
I watch.
I wait.
I see how things unfold before I decide it's really time to change strategy.

Think of me like the friend who doesn't say much at first. I'm not hovering or panicking. I'm just watching, reading the vibe, making sure you're good.

I've got you.
I always have.

And listen, I'm not asking you to decode every sensation. I'm not trying to become another thing on your to-do list.

I just need us on speaking terms.

When you know I'm here, and that nothing in your body has been acting solo, you don't have to work so hard to hold everything together.

That's my job.

Sharing load.
Distributing effort.
Keeping things from piling up in one place, so one area doesn't have to carry what belongs to the whole body.

Honestly? I'm the best friend you didn't know you had.

So... girl. Let's talk.

—

Note: The body operates through myofascial continuity, a network where parts are linked rather than separate. Movement and load don't stay confined to one spot; they're shared across regions, traveling along coordinated lines. This is why working on one area can create change somewhere else, and why tension doesn't always stay where it begins. This model of continuity has been mapped in fascial research, including the work of Thomas Myers.

We've Both Been Carrying This

We need to name something important.

We've been carrying life together, more than you might realize.

You might think this conversation is about tension. Or posture. Or the way your breath gets a little shallow when life gets busy.

But the truth is, we've been doing something much bigger than that.

Not just the obvious things—the schedule, the roles, the responsibilities, the decisions that needed to be made quickly and held quietly—but the subtler weight underneath it all.

The staying ready.
The adapting on the fly.
Staying alert even when you're technically resting.
Staying braced long after the moment passes.

It shows up like this:

Answering one more message before you sit down.
Finishing the task before you let yourself exhale.
Eating standing up because sitting felt indulgent.
Scanning the room without realizing it.
Answering before the sentence is finished—already braced for what you assumed was coming.
Sleeping light, half-listening, just in case.

You didn't just carry life in your mind.

You carried it in tissue.

It took shape in the way your body held itself—breath shallowing, stomach tightening, a leg that bounced when everything else stayed still.

You've been keeping things together.

And while you were doing that, I was working behind the scenes.

When something couldn't be dropped yet, it was held—quietly, in the background.
When something needed steadiness before there was clarity, structure formed.
Hello, bracing. Hello, hunching.
When pausing felt unsafe or impractical, movement continued—because stopping didn't feel like an option.

That's not pathology.

That's partnership.

The thing is, no one pulled you aside and told you this was happening. That your body was adapting with you. That your tissues were learning your patterns, your structure quietly reorganizing around what you were carrying.

So it probably felt like you were carrying it alone.

You weren't.

You thought you were holding it together.
I was making sure nothing collapsed when it all piled up.

And because it worked, those strategies stayed in place longer than you might expect.

Bodies are loyal like that.

Now there's room to notice it.

This conversation isn't here to undo the past.
It's here to update the relationship.

Because we're going to keep living in the same body, we might as well work as a team.

You don't have to stop being capable.
You don't have to stop being reliable.
You don't have to stop showing up.

But you don't have to carry it the same way.

As we keep going, I'm going to point out some familiar places this holding and bracing shows up.

We'll start with the obvious ones,
the places that learned to step in early and stay late—
the overachievers, the first responders.

Like your shoulders.

They've been very helpful.

We should probably talk about them.

—

Note: Fascia adapts to what it's repeatedly asked to do. Over time, sustained tension, load, and repeated responses can shape how tissue organizes and shares effort across the body. These patterns can linger even after the original demand has passed. What's been carried tends to leave a trace—not as a flaw, but as a form of adaptation, as explored in anatomical research by Carla Stecco.

Girl. Why Are Your Shoulders Up There.

Okay, but seriously—
why are your shoulders *up there*?

No really.

Like...
What meeting are they attending?
What are they preparing for?
Who told them to clock in early and stay late?

Because right now?

Nothing that urgent is happening.

Your shoulders have a habit of arriving early. They volunteer. They anticipate. They're very helpful.

A little too helpful.

They saw responsibility coming and said, "Got it."

They didn't wait to be asked.
They didn't wait for clarification.
They just clocked in.

Honestly, they've got a strong work ethic.

Which brings me to this:

Your shoulders are giving full 1980s shoulder pad vibes.
Power blazer.
Boardroom confidence.
"I will handle this" posture.

Boss babe. But... structural.

And listen—those shoulder pads existed for a reason.
They said, "I'm capable. I'm in charge. I belong here."

Your shoulders learned the same lesson.

They learned that lifting, bracing, and staying ready made things work. So they stayed in that shape. That's why they're still doing it.

And if you're noticing this right now—your shoulders inching up as you read, your neck tightening like it's concentrating—that's not ironic.

That's on brand.

These areas brace when you're focused or responsible, managing something quietly in your head.

They're first responders.

They see effort coming and say, "Say less."

Which is impressive.

Also... exhausting.

The thing is, styles change.

What worked in one era doesn't always need to run the show forever.

The power blazer had a moment.
It served its purpose.
And eventually, it got retired.
Things shifted.

Your shoulders haven't gotten that memo yet.

They're still dressed for a decade that asked you to hold a lot together.

So if they're still up there right now, it's old competence hanging around.

We'll come back to this.

Your shoulders have been saying a lot.

And they're not the only ones.

—

Note: The neck and shoulders often act as early stabilizers when the body senses effort or strain—in part because the neck houses the brainstem connection and the shoulders frame your sightline, making them the body's natural first line of response. With repeated patterns of bracing and load, and ongoing input from the nervous system, fascia adapts, shaping how the body holds itself in anticipation and letting these patterns settle into baseline tension long after the original moment.

It's a Group Chat. Everyone Has Thoughts.

Okay. So—it's not just the shoulders.

I know it looked like it was just them for a minute. They do tend to be the loudest in public. Very visible. Very committed.

But the truth is?

There's a group chat.

And everyone's in it.

Neck's here.
Jaw never left.
Chest is lurking.
Hips read everything but don't always respond.
Breath pops in and out like, "sorry—just catching up."

Your body doesn't wait for a full paragraph before it moves. It responds to what's happening, not what should be happening.

And the nervous system?

She's running the chat.
Setting the pace.
Adjusting the volume.

When things feel steady, the messages slow down.
When something changes, the thread gets active.

Tightness.
Buzzing.
Heaviness.
Numbness.
That low-grade *ugh* you couldn't quite name.

Those weren't interruptions.

They were updates.

She caught something shifting. Everyone adjusted.

And here's what matters:

You've been reading this fluently the whole time.

You knew when something felt off.
You knew when your body said, "*Not like this.*"
You knew when to brace and when to pull back—even
if you couldn't explain it neatly.

That's actually everything.

You've been reading a language no one ever formally taught you.

—

Note: When several areas seem to react at once, it reflects how the body communicates and organizes support across systems. Fascia helps transmit and distribute these changes, which is why adjustments often appear in more than one place at a time.

Seen. Cleared. Proceed.

And if you could see the thread, it might look something like this:

Shoulders:
okay why am I up again

Jaw:
you clocked something first

Shoulders:
I KNOW
I didn't even mean to
it just... happened

Neck:
hold on
checking the room...

Breath:
hey sorry just got here
what's the vibe

Chest:
alert
not alarmed
just... alert

Hips:
noted

Fascia:
everyone pause
let's wait a beat

(typing indicator appears... stops... appears again)

Nervous System:
scanning

Jaw:
yep
that tracks

Shoulders:
copy
holding but lighter

Neck:
micro-adjustments only

Breath:

slowing intake

Chest:
pressure steady
no escalation

Brows:
why am *I* tense

Jaw:
you're reading expressions
social math in progress

Brows:
ugh
hate that job
but okay

Stomach:
are we in trouble or just hungry

Fascia:
checking context

Breath:
it's noon

Stomach:
oh
my bad

carry on

(pause)

(things settle)

Nervous System:
clear
we're good

Fascia:
received
redistributing now

Shoulders:
dropping
didn't realize I was waiting

Neck:
same
release complete

Breath:
wow
that was smooth

Chest:
settled

Hips:

logged
for future reference

(the chat quiets, but stays open)

Auto-Save Was On

This is something worth saying now.

Auto-save was on.

Things were moving fast—you were busy surviving, and I was doing what I always do when life starts asking more questions than anyone can answer.

I kept what worked.

When something helps you get through a moment, I take note.
When a response steadies you, I remember.
When a way of holding yourself makes things more manageable, I keep it.

That time you realized staying composed got you through a situation with less fallout?
Saved.

The way holding your breath helped you stay steady when things felt uncertain?
Logged.

That subtle brace that helped you feel prepared walking into rooms where you had to read the air?
Stored.

Also stored:

Not just what you did—how your body learned to do it.

Going emotionally quiet so you could keep the peace.
Making yourself smaller in moments that didn't feel safe to take up space.
Keeping things steady—even when your body absorbed the cost.
That constant low-level readiness you didn't consciously choose.

You adapted beautifully.
Not randomly. Not excessively. Specifically.

Because those responses worked—even a little—I kept them.

Just in case.
For later.
Until things felt more spacious.

Some of it stayed active, ready to step in if something felt familiar. Some of it eased when it wasn't needed in the same way anymore.

The nervous system bookmarks what helps you feel safer. I adapt to support it.

But now you're starting to notice what's been staying ready.

Oh. That helped once.
Oh. That's why I do that.
Oh. That makes sense.

Sensations. Patterns.
Familiar responses that show up when the moment doesn't quite call for them anymore.

And the beauty is—that's what changes it.

Once something is seen, it doesn't have to stay active.

It can step back.

You might feel that as a small exhale.
A little less effort in places that had been quietly working all day.

—

Note: Adaptive behaviors—repeated protective responses to stress or uncertainty—can become familiar patterns in both the nervous system and the body. Because fascia responds to repeated tension and movement patterns, these adaptations can influence how the body organizes and maintains support over time. These patterns aren't stored as literal memories in tissue, but repeated inputs can shape patterns the body becomes more likely to anticipate and repeat.

Update in Progress

As you look at what stayed,
  you might begin to notice what doesn't have to
anymore.

Have you noticed how sometimes your body softens
before you do anything about it?

Your shoulders drop the second you're alone. Your
breath deepens when a room goes quiet. That sigh slips
out when the day finally loosens its grip on you.

You didn't plan that.

It just does.

I respond to context more than intention.
I'm always in conversation with your nervous system. As
it tracks what's happening around you, I adjust support in
real time.

You can tell yourself to relax all you want, but if part of you is still braced for interruption, your body won't believe you.

But the moment you close the door, drop your bag, and realize you're actually alone, something shifts without asking permission. Your shoulders lower. Your breath changes.

Not because you decided to soften, but because the context did.

And sometimes, that context is a person.

The one you don't have to brace around.
The one who doesn't rush you, read into you, or require you to hold everything together just to stay in the room.

Effort stops collecting in one place.

Support spreads out.

Tension that was doing a job starts to ease its grip.

And suddenly there's space again—
space to breathe, to think, to feel.
That space has a purpose. It's margin—the room your body uses to adjust, recover, and respond without urgency.

That's intelligence at work.

Your body knows how to shift when it has what it needs. You've been giving it that support all along. Sometimes without realizing it.

Even in small ways.

You light a candle without planning to. You run the bath a little fuller than necessary. You pour the good tea and actually sit down with it. You slip outside for five minutes of quiet and call it nothing, but your body called it necessary.

How you respond to yourself is part of what makes that possible.

So if you notice your shoulders drop when you walk in, or something loosens when the house finally goes quiet—don't rush past that. That's not nothing. That's your body updating in real time.

Maybe even let yourself set things down for a moment. The thoughts, the to-do list, the mental tabs you've been carrying. Notice what your body does with that.

Notice what it feels like when something lets go.

That's how things begin to change.

—

Note: Fascial tone is influenced by environment and perceived safety. These responses aren't something you can fully control on command. They emerge through constant communication between sensory input and the nervous system. When conditions shift, the body often adjusts with them. This creates margin—physiological space that allows for variability, recovery, and more room for different responses. These dynamics are explored in fascia research, including the work of Robert Schleip.

A Quick Orientation

You've been living with me your whole life. Might as well know a few things about how I work.

Not as rules.
More like... preferences.

Think of this as a quick reference.
Or a "good to know" list for the body you already live in.

Fascia at a Glance

I work well with contact: sustained pressure, gentle traction, warmth, rhythm.
That's why massage, stretching, slow movement, or even leaning into the back of a chair can change how your body feels.
It gives me something to respond to.

Forcing doesn't work well with me. Small and steady gets further than dramatic effort—which I know is annoying to hear, but here we are.

I distribute load.
I'm not built to hold everything in one place. When support is available, I spread effort out. When it isn't, I concentrate it where I can.

Rushing usually creates more holding, not less. I respond best when there's enough room to notice what's happening.

The nervous system and I work together, but we're not the same thing.
The nervous system is fast. It scans, alerts, reacts.
I'm slower. I organize, support, and stabilize.

We're closely linked, in constant communication—but we have different jobs.
If the nervous system is reading the room, I'm rearranging the furniture.

I like warmth, hydration, and movement that feels safe, especially the slow, varied kind.

That's why slow, intentional movement—the kind that doesn't rush past sensation—feels different.
It gives you time to notice.

To stay with what's happening instead of moving past
it.

Or honestly,
swaying a little in the kitchen when you're alone.
Letting your body move to a song without
choreography or purpose.

Fast, repetitive, output-driven movement has its place.
But slow, purposeful movement is often where I soften
first.
It gives your body more to work with.

Walking counts too.
The kind where your arms swing, your ribs rotate, and
your feet roll through the ground.

I show up a lot in your feet.
Rolling, stretching, and moving with intention can
create shifts throughout your whole body.

I also like variety. Changing positions, reaching,
twisting, bending.
Nothing extreme. Movement that reminds the body it
has options.

You'll notice me through sensation—shifts, ease,
resistance, the sense that something is or isn't moving
freely.

I hold until the body has enough safety and space to do otherwise.

If something feels tight, braced, or heavy, it's usually because I'm still doing a job I once had to do.

Sometimes, simply seeing that is enough for something to shift.

When you move, whether it's strength or cardio, leave a little space for me too.
To move slower sometimes.
To follow what you feel.

When something feels stuck, remember: I need hydration—and movement slow enough to reach the places that haven't let go yet.

Here's something worth knowing.
I don't hydrate the way you might think.
It's not just about drinking water.

Movement is what actually circulates fluid through my tissue—compression and release, like a sponge.
The more you move, the more I can do my job.

Think full, intentional range—arms, legs, hips—moving in ways that let things open gradually.

That's part of how I stay fluid.

When I'm fluid, I move with you more easily.

Keep me in mind.
Part of the friend group.

—

Note: Fascia hydrates primarily through movement, compression, and release rather than fluid intake alone. When tissue is compressed and released, fluid circulates through it, keeping it responsive and mobile. When fascia is under-moved or chronically compressed, it can start to feel sticky or restricted. Drinking water supports this process, but movement is what actually delivers hydration to the tissue. As a dynamic, responsive tissue, fascia helps share load, coordinate movement, and support how the body senses itself from within. It responds to movement and contact while also being influenced by the nervous system and overall context. Because it forms a continuous network throughout the body—including areas like the feet—changes in one place can affect the system as a whole. These roles have been explored across fascia research, including the work of David Lesondak.

On Speaking Terms

So, girl—

thanks for listening.

This body has been through a lot.

And now that we're on speaking terms, the way we carry life might feel a little less confusing.

Before we close, just remember this:

Every time you sensed something was off before you could name it, every time you kept going when everything was asking more than you had, every time your body found a way to carry what felt uncarriable—

that wasn't just survival.

That was intelligence.

That was your body doing exactly what it was designed
to do.

And also?
You don't have to earn rest.
Needs aren't something you qualify for.
You're allowed to slow down.

You're worth that.

—*Still here.*

From Me to You

Hey love,

If you made it here, something in you was ready for this conversation. And that matters.

My hope is that the next time your body speaks—a tightening, a shift, an exhale that comes out of nowhere—you recognize it. Not as something to fix or override, but as information. As intelligence. As a system that has been working for you this whole time, even when it didn't feel that way.

You weren't broken. You were never broken.

You were just waiting to be introduced.

You don't need to keep this book open to keep the conversation going. Your body knows how to continue it. It always has.

If You're Curious: The Science Behind It

If you're someone who enjoys exploring the science behind the body, fascia is an area that has seen significant growth in research over the past two decades.

It plays a role in movement, force transmission, proprioception (your body's sense of where it is in space), and its interaction with the nervous system.

This isn't a scientific deep dive.
Just a way of putting language to what you've already been noticing.

If you're interested in learning more, the work of these researchers has helped expand our understanding of fascia:

Robert Schleip—fascia and its connection to the nervous system
Thomas Myers—mapping fascial connections throughout the body (*Anatomy Trains*)

Carla Stecco—anatomical research on fascia structure and function

David Lesondak—accessible fascia education and its role in everyday experience

The research is still evolving.

But what's becoming clear is that fascia plays a meaningful role in how we move, feel, and experience our bodies.

And that includes the subtle patterns you've been noticing.

The tension.

The shifts.

The way it responds before you think about it.

Which means the way you've been experiencing your body...

isn't random.